TOOLS FOR CAREGIVERS

- **ATOS:** 0.8
- **GRL:** C
- **WORD COUNT:** 63

- **CURRICULUM CONNECTIONS:** animals, directions, nature, opposites

Skills to Teach

- **HIGH-FREQUENCY WORDS:** and, are, in, is, its, out, the, these, this
- **CONTENT WORDS:** baby, bird, den, dolphins, eel, fox, fun, hole, nest, pouch, shell, turtle, water
- **PUNCTUATION:** exclamation points, periods
- **WORD STUDY:** /f/, spelled ph (dolphins); long /e/, spelled y (baby); long /e/, spelled ee (eel); /ow/, spelled ou (out, pouch); r-controlled vowels (bird, turtle); /sh/, spelled sh (shell)
- **TEXT TYPE:** information report

Before Reading Activities

- Read the title and give a simple statement of the main idea.
- Have students "walk" though the book and talk about what they see in the pictures.
- Introduce new vocabulary by having students predict the first letter and locate the word in the text.
- Discuss any unfamiliar concepts that are in the text.

After Reading Activities

The text mentions different animals that are in and out of their homes or elements. In and out are directions. They are also opposites. Can the readers think of other animals that go inside something, such as the bird that goes in and out of its nest? Ask the readers about the objects around them. Are they in a school? A library? A home? What is outside of the school, library, or home?

Tadpole Books are published by Jump!, 5357 Penn Avenue South, Minneapolis, MN 55419, www.jumplibrary.com

Copyright ©2019 Jump!. International copyright reserved in all countries. No part of this book may be reproduced in any form without written permission from the publisher.

Editor: Jenna Trnka **Designer:** Anna Peterson

Photo Credits: r.classen/Shutterstock, cover; yevgeniy11/Shutterstock, 1; Chiyacat/Shutterstock, 2–3, 4–5 (background), 16tr; Mikelane45/Dreamstime, 4–5 (bird); avs_lt/iStock, 6–7, 16tl; Smileus/iStock, 8, 16bl; Bradley Blackburn/Shutterstock, 9 (mom); LifetimeStock/Shutterstock, 9 (baby); Dan Exton/Shutterstock, 10, 11 (background), 16tm; fenkieandreas/Shutterstock, 11 (eel); princessdlaf/iStock, 12, 13, 16bm; Willyam Bradberry/Shutterstock, 14, 15, 16br.

Library of Congress Cataloging-in-Publication Data
Names: Kenan, Tessa, author.
Title: In and out / by Tessa Kenan.
Description: Minneapolis, MN: Jump!, Inc., (2019) | Series: Comparing directions | Includes index.
Identifiers: LCCN 2018020599 (print) | LCCN 2018024706 (ebook) | ISBN 9781641284288 (ebook) |
ISBN 9781641284264 (hardcover : alk. paper) | ISBN 9781641284271 (pbk.)
Subjects: LCSH: Orientation—Juvenile literature. | Polarity—Juvenile literature.
Classification: LCC BF299.O7 (ebook) | LCC BF299.O7 K46 2018 (print) | DDC 152.1/882—dc23
LC record available at https://lccn.loc.gov/2018020599

COMPARING DIRECTIONS

IN AND OUT

by Tessa Kenan

TABLE OF CONTENTS

tadpole
books

IN AND OUT

nest

This bird is
in the nest.

This bird is out!

den ······▶

This fox is in the den.

This fox is out!

pouch

This baby is in the pouch.

baby

This baby is out!

hole

This eel is in the hole.

This eel is out!

shell

This turtle
is in its shell.

This turtle is out!

water

These dolphins are in the water.

These are out! Fun!

WORDS TO KNOW

den

hole

nest

pouch

shell

water

INDEX